PRAYERSCRIPTS
Speaking God's Word Back To You

DELIVER from THE ENEMY

30 Days of Prayers for
CALLING ON GOD'S POWER FOR FREEDOM, RESCUE, AND LASTING VICTORY

CYRIL OPOKU

Deliver from the Enemy: Calling on God's Power for Freedom, Rescue, and Lasting Victory

© 2025 Cyril Opoku. *PrayerScripts*. All rights reserved.

Published by *Quest Publications*

ISBN: 978-1-988439-79-2

Cover design by *Quest Publications (questpublications@outlook.com)*

Unless otherwise indicated, all Scripture quotations are taken from the World English Bible WEB, which is in the public domain. For more information, visit: www.worldenglish.bible

This book is a work of devotional encouragement. It is not intended to replace biblical study, pastoral counsel, or professional therapy.

Printed in the United States of America.

First Edition: August 2025

For more books like this, visit *PrayerScripts:* https://prayerscripts.org

CONTENTS

PREFACE

Many are the afflictions of the righteous, but Yahweh
delivers him out of them all.
—Psalm 34:19 WEB

Deliverance is at the heart of God's covenant with His people. From Genesis to Revelation, we see His hand stretched out to rescue, redeem, and restore those who call upon His name. The story of salvation itself is a story of deliverance—freedom from sin, victory over Satan, and triumph through the blood of Jesus.

This book was written because every believer faces moments when the pressure of life seems unbearable, when spiritual enemies rise with fury, and when breakthrough feels far out of reach. In those moments, the greatest weapon we possess is God's Word on our lips, spoken in prayer with bold faith. Scripture does not simply inspire—it delivers, it defends, it destroys the works of darkness.

Deliver from the Enemy is not just a collection of verses and prayers; it is an invitation to step into God's power of rescue for yourself and your family. Each prayer is drawn directly from Scripture and infused with prophetic fire to equip you for battle, to call on God's saving strength, and to walk in the victory Christ has already secured.

As you read, declare, and pray these words, expect transformation. Expect chains to be broken, doors to be opened, and battles to be won. The God who delivered yesterday is the same God who will deliver you today. This is your moment to rise, to call on Him with confidence, and to see His mighty hand at work in your life.

Ready at His command,
Cyril O. *(Illinois, August 2025)*

INTRODUCTION

There comes a moment in every believer's journey when the battle is no longer avoidable. Darkness presses in, the enemy pursues, and the storms rage with no sign of letting up. In that moment, one truth must thunder in your spirit: **God alone is your Deliverer.**

This book was born out of the fire of warfare and the cry for freedom. It is not a manual of empty words, but a prophetic arsenal drawn from the eternal Word of God. Within these pages, you will encounter Scriptures that have shattered chains, silenced oppressors, and overturned the works of darkness for generations. Coupled with Spirit-breathed prayers, they are designed to ignite your faith, sharpen your spiritual authority, and usher you into undeniable victory.

Deliverance is not a suggestion—it is your covenant right through the blood of Jesus. The same God who parted the Red Sea, who walked with His children through fire, who silenced the fury of lions, and who struck down entire armies for the sake of His people is still the God who fights for you today. His power has not diminished. His arm has not grown weak. And His promise of rescue remains unshakable.

As you journey through these prayers, prepare for breakthrough. Expect chains to snap. Expect spiritual enemies to bow. Expect songs of deliverance to rise over your life and family. For the Lord, mighty in battle, is rising to defend you, and through Him, you will walk in freedom, rescue, and lasting victory.

How to Use This Book

This is not a book to be rushed through. Each of the 30 prayers is structured as a daily prayer journey, combining the Word of God with prophetic, Spirit-led intercession. Here's how you can make the most of it:

1. **Start with the Scripture** – Each prayer begins with a verse from the World English Bible (WEB). Read it slowly and aloud, letting the Word sink into your heart.

2. **Declare the Word** – Meditate on the key truth in the verse, affirming it as God's unchanging promise.

3. **Pray with Authority** – Use the written prayer as a guide. Speak it boldly, personally, and with conviction. Replace "I" with your name or the names of loved ones as needed.

4. **Journal Insights** – Keep a notebook nearby. Write down any impressions, warnings, or directions you sense from the Holy Spirit.

5. **Build a Rhythm** – Pray one Scripture each day, or linger longer on those that strike you deeply. Repetition builds sharpness, and sharpness builds victory.

Whether you walk through these prayers privately in your devotional time, with your family, or in a small group, the key is consistency. Each prayer is a sword in your hand—use it faithfully.

DAY 1

THE CRY OF THE RIGHTEOUS

"The righteous cry, and Yahweh hears, and delivers them
out of all their troubles."
— Psalm 34:17 WEB

Faithful Deliverer, I lift my voice with confidence, declaring that
when I cry out, You hear me. You are not distant, nor are You silent,
but You are near to the cries of the righteous. I proclaim that every
trouble sent against me and my family is met with the mighty hand
of God who rescues and redeems.

Lord, I thank You that no affliction, no storm, and no attack of the
enemy is too strong for Your power to overcome. Where chains of
oppression seek to bind, You break them. Where arrows of fear are
launched, You shield me. Where the adversary lays snares, You lift
me above them. My Deliverer is mighty, and His salvation cannot
fail.

I cry out over my home today: deliver us from the plots of darkness,
from every trap of temptation, from every scheme designed to
derail us. Rescue us from hidden attacks, from secret snares, and
from the powers that seek our downfall. Expose the hand of the
enemy and rescue us by Your outstretched arm.

I declare boldly that I will not remain in captivity. My Deliverer has
come, my cry has been heard, and my family is free. Troubles may
come, but none can hold me, for the Lord delivers me from them
all. In Jesus' name, Amen.

DAY 2

RESCUED BY HIS REFUGE

He who dwells in the secret place of the Most High will rest in the shadow of the Almighty. I will say of Yahweh, "He is my refuge and my fortress; my God, in whom I trust." For he will deliver you from the snare of the fowler, and from the deadly pestilence. He will cover you with his feathers. Under his wings you will take refuge. His faithfulness is your shield and rampart.
— Psalm 91:1-4 WEB

Most High God, I run into the shelter of Your presence today. You are my fortress, my hiding place, my shield, and my strong deliverer. I declare that no trap set by the enemy shall capture me or my family, for You cover us with the shadow of Your wings.

Lord, deliver us from every snare of the fowler—the hidden plots, the unseen schemes, the subtle traps of destruction. Rescue us from the pestilence that stalks in darkness, from sickness, fear, calamity, and the arrows of oppression. I proclaim that no ambush of the enemy shall prosper against us, for You are our shield and buckler.

Father, as we rest in Your secret place, guard our minds from torment, our bodies from harm, and our souls from despair. Expose every hidden danger and snatch us from the hands of those who seek our downfall. Let no curse, enchantment, or wicked agenda succeed against my household.

I declare that my family is safe under Your wings. We are rescued from evil's grip and preserved in the safety of Your faithfulness. You alone are our refuge, and in You we find peace and protection from all harm.

In Jesus' name, Amen.

DAY 3

CRY FOR RESCUE

"Then they cry to Yahweh in their trouble, he saves them out of their distresses. He sends his word, and heals them, and delivers them from their graves."
—Psalm 107:19-20 WEB

Delivering God, Redeemer of my soul, I lift my cry to You on behalf of myself and my family. You are the One who hears us in our distress, and You are mighty to deliver us from every pit the enemy has dug. I declare today that every chain of oppression is broken, and every snare of destruction is exposed.

Lord, release Your Word like a sharp sword into every area of bondage. Let Your Word heal the wounded, strengthen the weary, and restore the broken places in my life and in my family's lives. Let every shadow of death be pushed back by the light of Your salvation.

I decree that we are no longer bound by fear, sickness, or torment. Every spiritual grave where the enemy has tried to bury our hope, our joy, or our purpose is opened by Your resurrection power. Let deliverance be our portion, and let freedom ring loudly in our household.

Father, arise as the Mighty Deliverer, rescuing us from the oppression of the enemy. You are faithful to save, and I will not be moved by the lies of the adversary. I receive healing, freedom, and restoration for my family today. In Jesus' name, Amen.

DAY 4

THE LORD RESCUES ME

And the Lord will deliver me from every evil work, and will preserve me for his heavenly Kingdom; to whom be the glory forever and ever. Amen.
— 2 Timothy 4:18 WEB

Faithful Deliverer, I lift my hands in trust to You, my Defender and Shield. You have promised to rescue me from every evil work, and I lay hold of that promise today. No scheme of hell, no plot of man, no hidden snare shall overpower the keeping power of the Lord.

Father, deliver my family from the traps set against us. Where the enemy seeks to bring sickness, let healing arise. Where he plots confusion, let peace abound. Where he whispers fear, let courage stand tall. You, O Lord, are our Preserver, guarding our lives unto Your eternal Kingdom.

I renounce every assignment of destruction and decree deliverance over my household. Evil cannot entangle us, for You break every chain. You snatch us out of snares, You lift us above pits, You shelter us from storms. The wicked may rise, but they cannot prevail, for You always provide a way of escape.

Thank You, Lord, for preserving our faith, our destiny, and our future. My family is covered, and we are carried by Your mighty hand into victory. All glory belongs to You forever.

In Jesus' name, Amen.

DAY 5

THE LORD RESCUES

"The Lord knows how to deliver the godly out of temptation and to keep the unrighteous under punishment for the day of judgment."
— 2 Peter 2:9 WEB

Faithful Deliverer, my Shield and my Fortress, I cry out in confidence that You know how to rescue me from every snare. Your wisdom is infinite, and Your power unfailing. No trap is too hidden, no chain too strong, no enemy too great for You to break.

Father, deliver me and my family from every temptation of compromise, every lure of deception, and every scheme designed to lead us astray. Keep us secure in Your righteousness, sheltered in Your truth, and steadfast in Your covenant. Rescue us from the pits dug by our adversaries and set our feet upon the solid rock of Your Word.

I proclaim that the hand of the Lord reaches into every circumstance of danger, oppression, or captivity and pulls us out. Temptations lose their grip, and snares of the wicked are rendered ineffective. My family is hidden in the secret place of the Most High, untouchable by the assaults of the enemy.

Lord, keep the unrighteous under Your judgment, but let Your mercy rest upon us. As You delivered Noah, Lot, and Daniel, so You will deliver me. This is my confidence: I am preserved by Your mighty hand, guarded day and night by Your unfailing power. In Jesus' name, Amen.

DAY 6

ESCAPE IN GOD'S FAITHFULNESS

"No temptation has taken you except what is common to man. God is faithful, who will not allow you to be tempted above what you are able, but will with the temptation also make the way of escape, that you may be able to endure it."
— 1 Corinthians 10:13 WEB

O Faithful Father, Covenant-Keeping God, I lift my voice in triumph today! You are my Deliverer, my Keeper, and the One who never abandons me to the snares of the wicked one. Even when the enemy surrounds me with temptations, snares, and afflictions designed to entrap me, Your faithfulness stands as my shield. You will never allow me or my household to be crushed beyond our capacity, for You are the God of escape, the God of intervention, the God of divine way out.

I declare in the Spirit: no chain of temptation, no cycle of bondage, no inherited curse, and no demonic snare shall prevail over me. You have appointed a path of freedom and victory. I claim it for myself and my family. The schemes of the devil are broken; the deceit of the enemy is exposed; every hidden trap is uncovered by the light of Christ.

Lord, I prophetically step into the escape route You have made. I step into liberty, into holiness, into victory. I decree that the escape of the Lord shall be visible in my life. No enemy shall triumph over me, for the faithful God fights for me.

By Your covenant faithfulness, my household is preserved. By Your mighty power, my children are delivered. By Your Spirit, we walk free of oppression, strong in holiness, untouchable by the power of sin. I will not be ensnared, for You have decreed escape.

In Jesus' name, Amen.

DAY 7

REFUGE IN TROUBLED TIMES

"God is our refuge and strength, a very present help in trouble."
— Psalm 46:1 WEB

Almighty God, my Fortress and Deliverer, I lift my heart in worship and war. You are my impregnable refuge, my place of safety, and my shield against the forces of darkness. Though storms may rage, though battles may arise, I stand firm because my Deliverer is with me. You are not distant, but ever present—ready, near, and mighty to rescue.

I decree that my life and family are hidden in the stronghold of the Most High. Every assault of the wicked, every arrow of fear, every weapon of destruction shall fall powerless against us. The enemy may seek to overwhelm, but You, O God, arise as our strength. You deliver us from fear, from despair, from captivity.

O Lord, I declare in faith that trouble will not consume us, because Your presence is our covering. You go before us, behind us, and around us like walls of fire. In Your presence, demonic powers shatter. In Your refuge, the wicked are scattered. No siege of darkness can breach the fortress of our Deliverer.

Therefore, I will not fear. My family will not be shaken. We stand delivered, protected, and untouchable because the Ever-Present Help is with us. Our refuge is not in man, not in our strength, but in the Deliverer who saves to the uttermost. In Jesus' name, Amen.

DAY 8

CALL AND BE RESCUED

"Call on me in the day of trouble. I will deliver you, and
you will honor me."
— Psalm 50:15 WEB

O God of Deliverance, I lift my cry to You today! You are the One
who answers from the heavens, the One whose arm is mighty to
save, the One who never abandons those who call upon Your name.
I invoke Your power over every trouble, every scheme of darkness,
and every attack against my destiny and my family.

I declare prophetically: the day of trouble shall not swallow me. The
fires of adversity shall not consume me. For when I call, You deliver!
When I lift my voice, You break the chains! When I cry out in the
night, You split the heavens and come down to rescue me.

Father, I renounce fear and embrace faith. I declare that no matter
what rises against me, You are stronger. My household is delivered
from the bondage of sin, from the arrows of witchcraft, from the
traps of the wicked. We will not be victims but victors. Trouble will
not define us, deliverance will.

And Lord, as You rescue me, I pledge to honor You. My lips will
testify. My family will glorify. The nations will know that the God I
serve delivers without fail. Let my deliverance become a song of
worship and a testimony of Your greatness.

In Jesus' name, Amen.

DAY 9

SPEEDY DELIVERANCE AND RESCUE

"Bow down your ear to me. Deliver me speedily. Be to me
a strong rock, a house of defense to save me."
— Psalm 31:2 WEB

O Lord Most High, the Rock of Ages and my Mighty Fortress,
incline Your ear to my cry today! You are my unshakable refuge, the
immovable Rock of my salvation, and my defense against the
onslaught of darkness. I cry for speed, O God—let my deliverance
come swiftly like lightning against every enemy pursuing me and
my family.

I declare that every delayed answer, every postponed breakthrough,
every prolonged affliction is shattered by the speed of heaven's
intervention. Let every arrow of witchcraft be reversed in haste. Let
every trap of the enemy be destroyed instantly. As David cried for
quick rescue, so I decree divine acceleration over my life and family.

Lord, I declare You to be my strong rock and house of defense. In
You, my household is fortified. In You, we are unmovable. No
storm, no sorcery, no curse, no demonic council can penetrate the
defense You have set around us.

Therefore, I stand bold, declaring freedom for my household. I call
forth immediate healing, sudden breakthrough, and swift release
from every oppression. No delay shall hinder my deliverance. You,
O Lord, save me with power and speed.

In Jesus' name, Amen.

DAY 10

FREEDOM FOR THE CAPTIVES

"The Spirit of the Lord is on me, because he has anointed me to preach good news to the poor. He has sent me to heal the brokenhearted, to proclaim release to the captives, recovering of sight to the blind, to deliver those who are crushed."
— Luke 4:18 WEB

Spirit of the Living God, fall afresh on me! You have anointed me by the blood of Jesus to walk in the power of deliverance. I lift my voice today as one set free, proclaiming liberty over every area of bondage, every stronghold of oppression, every crushing weight of darkness over my life and family.

By the anointing, I decree: every chain is broken, every captive is released, every prison door is shattered. The enemy's grip over my household is destroyed. Generational curses are lifted. Oppression is silenced. Demonic blindness gives way to the light of Christ.

O God, let the anointing heal broken hearts in my family. Let the crushed be restored. Let every spirit of heaviness be replaced with garments of praise. I decree the proclamation of freedom rings in my home, in my bloodline, and in every place where the enemy has tried to cage us.

Today I walk in my prophetic destiny, declaring liberty to my children, my household, and my generations. By the Spirit of the

Lord, we are untouchable, unstoppable, and unshakable. The enemy's oppression is ended, and freedom reigns forevermore.

In Jesus' name, Amen.

DAY 11

CROWNED WITH DELIVERANCE

"and delivered him out of all his afflictions, and gave him favor and wisdom before Pharaoh king of Egypt. He made him governor over Egypt and all his house."
— Acts 7:10 WEB

Mighty Deliverer, You are the God who rescued Joseph from every affliction, lifted him above the pit, and enthroned him in a palace. Today, I call upon You with confidence, for You are the same yesterday, today, and forever. The power that raised Joseph out of bondage is the same power I invoke over my life and my household.

Lord, every chain of affliction the enemy has placed on my destiny, let it break by Your mighty hand. Just as You gave Joseph favor and wisdom, clothe me with supernatural favor that cannot be denied and wisdom that cannot be resisted. Where my enemies have plotted evil, let those very plots become stepping stones to promotion. Where affliction has sought to drown me, let Your strong right arm lift me into victory.

I decree that no power of darkness will keep me bound. I will not be a prisoner to fear, sickness, delay, or oppression. By Your authority, Lord, I am rising into rulership over every circumstance that once sought to bury me. My family will not be enslaved to generational battles; we are lifted by the covenant blood of Jesus into dominion and authority.

Father, as Joseph became a testimony of Your delivering power to the nations, let my life shine as evidence that no affliction can outlast Your anointing. Establish me as a testimony in my generation. Let my deliverance bring honor to Your name and shame to every adversary.

In Jesus' name, Amen.

DAY 12

TRANSFERRED INTO THE KINGDOM

"who delivered us out of the power of darkness, and translated us into the Kingdom of the Son of his love."
— Colossians 1:13 WEB

Righteous Redeemer, I exalt You for breaking the grip of darkness and bringing me into the Kingdom of Your beloved Son. Today I stand firm in the reality that no power of hell has legal right over my life or my family. We are citizens of light, redeemed and established in the dominion of Christ.

Lord, every shadow of darkness attempting to reassert itself over me is shattered now. Every demonic chain, every curse, every spirit of bondage seeking to pull me back into captivity, I reject and renounce in the name of Jesus. I declare that my household will not be governed by the powers of night, but by the radiance of the Kingdom of Your love.

Father, let the banner of the Blood of Jesus stand tall over us. I decree that confusion, fear, and oppression shall not reign in my home. Let Your Kingdom come in righteousness, peace, and joy in the Holy Spirit. Let angelic hosts surround my dwelling, and let every weapon of darkness dissolve before the fire of Your presence.

O God of Deliverance, I embrace the authority You have given me in Christ. I walk boldly in freedom, knowing that the power of darkness is broken forever. I proclaim generational liberation, that my children and descendants will live only under the covering of Your Kingdom.

In Jesus' name, Amen.

DAY 13

RESCUED FROM EVIL PRESENT AGE

"who gave himself for our sins, that he might deliver us out of this present evil age, according to the will of our God and Father."
— Galatians 1:4 WEB

Glorious Savior, You gave Yourself for me, not only to forgive my sins but to rescue me from the corruption and snares of this present evil age. Today, I rise in the power of Your finished work on the cross, declaring that my deliverance is not negotiable—it is secured by the blood of the Lamb.

Lord, I reject every system, every entanglement, every lure of this wicked age that seeks to drag me into destruction. I declare that my life, my mind, and my household are set apart for You. No agenda of hell, no temptation of the world, no deception of Satan will ensnare us. I proclaim freedom from the grip of compromise, addiction, and worldly enticements.

Father, let the fire of Your Spirit purge every hidden work of darkness in me. Let the world see that I belong to the Kingdom that cannot be shaken. Guard my family from the ideologies, cultures, and practices that war against Your truth. Raise a hedge of fire around us, that we may live holy and blameless until the day of Christ's appearing.

I boldly declare that Christ has delivered me from the evil tides of this generation. My feet are anchored in righteousness. My eyes are set on eternity. My destiny is sealed in God's will, and no power of this age can snatch me from His hand.

In Jesus' name, Amen.

DAY 14

THE GOD WHO DELIVERS

"Nebuchadnezzar spoke and said, 'Blessed be the God of
Shadrach, Meshach, and Abednego, who has sent his
angel, and delivered his servants who trusted in him, and
have changed the king's word, and have yielded their
bodies, that they might not serve nor worship any god,
except their own God.'"
— Daniel 3:28 WEB

Almighty Deliverer, I worship You as the God who answers by fire,
the One who sends His angels to rescue His own. You are the God
who honors those who trust You, and You never abandon those
who refuse to bow to the idols of this world. Today, I declare that I
and my family will bow to no other god but You, the Living God.

Lord, just as You delivered Shadrach, Meshach, and Abednego from
the fiery furnace, deliver me from every fire set by the enemy. Let
the flames of trial, persecution, and affliction serve only to
showcase Your power and not to consume me. Every word, decree,
or curse spoken against my life, let it be overturned by Your
sovereign authority.

I decree that no furnace of sickness, lack, or oppression shall
destroy me. Instead, like those Hebrew men, I will emerge without
the smell of smoke, untouched and unscarred. My life will testify to
kings and nations that there is no God who delivers like my God.

Father, strengthen me to yield my body, my will, and my life wholly to You. May every act of my obedience shine as a witness that You alone are worthy of worship. Let my deliverance provoke praise from the mouths of even my enemies, until they bow and acknowledge that You are Lord of all.

In Jesus' name, Amen.

DAY 15

SURROUNDED BY HEAVEN'S HOST

"He answered, 'Don't be afraid; for those who are with us are more than those who are with them.'"
— 2 Kings 6:16 WEB

Lord of Hosts, I lift my eyes to You, the Commander of angel armies. You have not left me alone, for Your invisible forces surround me and my household. Today, I refuse fear, for greater are those with me than those against me.

Father, open my spiritual eyes that I may see the vast host of heaven arrayed for my deliverance. Let every spirit of intimidation, panic, and doubt be crushed under the revelation of Your mighty presence. I decree that though the enemy plots, surrounds, and schemes, I will not be moved, for my Defender is strong and my Deliverer is near.

I declare that my family is encompassed by chariots of fire. Every arrow aimed at us shall be extinguished before it strikes. Every ambush of the wicked is dismantled before it forms. Where darkness advances, let Your blazing light push it back. Where fear whispers, let the shout of heaven's armies thunder louder.

O God, I rest in the assurance that I am not outnumbered, for You are my shield and exceeding great reward. The enemy shall scatter in seven directions, and my victory shall stand firm in the presence of Your angelic host.

In Jesus' name, Amen.

DAY 16

THE LORD MY STRONGHOLD

"Yahweh is good, a stronghold in the day of trouble; and
he knows those who take refuge in him."
—Nahum 1:7 WEB

O Lord, my Refuge and Fortress, I run into Your presence with holy
confidence. You are the stronghold of my life, the Rock that cannot
be shaken by storm or assault. When the enemy plots destruction,
I hide under the shadow of Your wings and am secured by Your
unfailing love. Because You know me, You shield me; because You
are good, You preserve me from the wicked schemes of darkness.

Father, I decree today that every trouble raised against my
household shall be swallowed up by the refuge of Your power. The
raging storms of affliction, the arrows of the adversary, and the
whispers of fear are silenced in Your stronghold. No evil spirit, no
demonic voice, no hidden snare can prevail against the fortress of
Your name. You are my tower of deliverance, and in You I am
untouchable.

Lord, let the floods of trouble be diverted away from me and my
family. Establish the walls of Your divine protection around our
lives, our health, our minds, and our destinies. Let Your goodness
pursue us daily, and let Your knowledge of us become a shield that
the wicked cannot penetrate.

I declare with faith: I will not be moved, I will not be broken, for the
Stronghold of the Lord is my dwelling place. The enemy is defeated,

his works are scattered, and his counsel is shattered, for Yahweh has spoken good concerning me.

In Jesus' name, Amen.

DAY 17

My Rock and Deliverer

"Yahweh is my rock, my fortress, and my deliverer; my God, my rock, in whom I take refuge; my shield, and the horn of my salvation, my high tower."
—Psalm 18:2 WEB

Mighty Deliverer, I exalt You as my Rock and Fortress. In the midst of battle, I cling to You as my sure foundation, unshakable and everlasting. You are the shield that quenches every fiery dart, the horn of salvation that breaks the power of the wicked, and the tower that lifts me above the snares of the enemy.

I declare today that no adversary can triumph over me, because my life is hidden in Christ and anchored in the Rock of Ages. Every satanic plot collapses before the strength of my Fortress. Every generational chain shatters before the horn of salvation. Every storm of destruction is calmed by the power of my Deliverer.

Lord, let Your shield encompass my family on every side. Cover our health, our future, and our calling with Your mighty hand. Raise me high above the reach of the wicked, where their arrows cannot touch me. Let every spiritual ambush fail, every demonic siege crumble, and every weapon forged against me return in shame to its sender.

Father, I confess boldly: I am not a victim but a victor, not a captive but the redeemed of the Lord. My feet are planted firmly on the Rock, my heart is guarded by the Fortress, and my destiny is carried by the Deliverer. Therefore, the plans of hell are powerless, and the blessings of heaven overflow upon me.

In Jesus' name, Amen.

DAY 18

RESCUED AGAIN AND AGAIN

"Who delivered us out of so great a death, and does
deliver; on whom we have set our hope that he will also
still deliver us."
—2 Corinthians 1:10 WEB

Faithful Father, Deliverer of my soul, I lift my voice in thanksgiving.
You have delivered me from the jaws of death, You are delivering
me in this very hour, and You will continue to deliver me until the
end of my days. My hope is set on You, the Eternal Rescuer, who
never grows weary and never fails.

O Lord, let every sentence of death written against me be erased by
the blood of Jesus. Let every plan of destruction, every shadow of
the grave, and every demonic assignment against my family be
nullified by Your eternal deliverance. You are the God who rescues
from seen and unseen dangers, from physical harm and spiritual
snares alike.

I decree that the cycles of affliction in my bloodline are broken. The
chains of fear, sickness, and oppression are shattered. The grave has
no hold over me, because Christ has triumphed, and His
resurrection power is my guarantee of continual deliverance.

Lord, as You delivered me yesterday, deliver me today, and deliver
me tomorrow. Let my testimony ring in the earth: that I serve a God
who rescues without fail. I refuse to fear the threats of the wicked,

for my life rests in the hands of the Eternal Rescuer who has promised to keep me.

I boldly declare: my past is redeemed, my present is protected, and my future is secured, for the God of deliverance watches over me and my household.

In Jesus' name, Amen.

DAY 19

Victory Through His Anointed

"Now I know that Yahweh saves his anointed. He will answer him from his holy heaven, with the saving strength of his right hand."
—Psalm 20:6 WEB

Lord God Almighty, my Covenant Keeper, I rejoice in the assurance of Your Word. You save Your anointed, and in Christ Jesus I am chosen, sealed, and consecrated. I lift my cry today knowing that You hear me from Your holy heaven, and You stretch forth Your mighty right hand to deliver.

Father, I declare that every voice of accusation raised against me shall be silenced by the strength of Your salvation. Every chain of bondage shall be broken by the power of Your right hand. Every battlefield where the enemy seeks to overwhelm me shall become the stage of Your great victory.

Arise, O Lord, with saving strength, and fight for my family. Rescue us from the snares of witchcraft, from the plots of wicked men, and from the arrows of invisible powers. Let the saving hand of the Almighty scatter every enemy camp and overturn every evil decree spoken against my life.

I stand today in the authority of Your anointing. Because I am Yours, I cannot be defeated. Because You are my God, I cannot be destroyed. With the strength of Your right hand, I am lifted into triumph. My voice shall forever testify that the Lord saves His anointed, and no power of hell can undo what God has established. In Jesus' name, Amen.

DAY 20

Deliver Me in Righteousness

"Deliver me in your righteousness, and rescue me. Turn your ear to me, and save me."
—Psalm 71:2 WEB

Righteous Father, I lift my cry to You, the Just Judge of all the earth. You alone are my Deliverer, the One who saves not by the strength of man, but by the holiness of Your nature. In Your righteousness, rescue me from the grip of the adversary and let salvation flow into every corner of my life.

Lord, bend Your ear to my prayer. Hear the cries of my heart for myself and my family. Arise against the oppressors that surround us in secret. Scatter every spirit of infirmity, every cloud of depression, every weight of oppression. Deliver us, O Lord, from the snares set in darkness and the traps hidden in daylight.

By Your righteousness, let every unjust affliction be overturned. Vindicate me where I have been falsely accused, defend me where I have been unjustly attacked, and lift me above the shame the enemy seeks to impose. Let Your righteousness shine as a banner over my household, proving that those who trust in the Lord shall never be put to shame.

Father, I decree that my deliverance is not in my own strength, but in Your unchanging faithfulness. You save me because You are righteous; You rescue me because You are good. Therefore, I rest secure, knowing that every battle ends in my victory and every storm turns into peace by Your saving power.

In Jesus' name, Amen.

DAY 21

SOWING TEARS, REAPING JOY

Those who sow in tears will reap in joy.
—Psalm 126:5 WEB

O God of covenant mercy, I lift my voice to You, the Restorer of Zion and the Deliverer of the brokenhearted. You are the One who turns mourning into dancing and heaviness into garments of praise. Today I declare that my tears will not be wasted, for You are the God who transforms pain into purpose, sorrow into singing, and bondage into breakthrough.

Lord, every seed I have sown in weeping—every night of travail, every cry of desperation, every burden carried in faith—let it be remembered before You. Deliver me and my household from every enemy that seeks to choke the harvest of joy. Break the chains of sorrow, and scatter the spirits of oppression that war against my peace. Where the adversary has planted despair, I call forth a divine exchange: joy unspeakable and full of glory.

Father, let the tears that have watered the ground of my destiny now germinate into testimonies. Let every delay be turned to acceleration, every shame to honor, and every captivity to freedom. Deliver me from the snares of the wicked and cause my family to walk in the fullness of Your joy.

I decree that our days of sorrow are numbered, and our season of rejoicing is here. The enemy cannot keep us bound in grief, for You,

O Lord, are our Deliverer and Restorer. Let laughter spring forth in our mouths and songs of victory in our hearts.

In Jesus' name, Amen.

DAY 22

DELIVER US FROM EVIL

Bring us not into temptation, but deliver us from the evil
one. For yours is the Kingdom, the power, and the glory
forever. Amen.
—Matthew 6:13 WEB

Heavenly Father, Ruler of heaven and earth, I come before You as a child in need of Your strong deliverance. You are the God of all power, the King whose dominion knows no end. I call on Your holy name to deliver me, my family, and all that concerns us from the clutches of the evil one.

Lord, shield us from the snares of temptation, from the subtle strategies of darkness that seek to derail our destinies. By Your mighty hand, cut off every wicked assignment, every evil decree, every spiritual arrow fired against our lives. Rescue us from the plots of the adversary, for only in You do we find safety.

Father, let Your kingdom power surround my home like a fortress. Let Your glory drive away every demonic presence, every oppressive spirit, and every force of hell seeking to invade our peace. As You have all authority in heaven and earth, exercise Your dominion over every enemy voice speaking against our future.

Today I declare: no trap of the enemy will prosper, no chain will hold us, no curse will prevail. By the blood of Jesus Christ, I walk in freedom, in victory, and in divine protection. The power of evil is broken, and the glory of God is my covering. In Jesus' name, Amen.

DAY 23

He Answers in Trouble

He will call on me, and I will answer him. I will be with
him in trouble. I will deliver him, and honor him.
—Psalm 91:15 WEB

Faithful Deliverer, I cry out to You today, the God who answers
when Your people call. You are the Defender of the helpless, the
Shield of the righteous, and the Mighty One who saves. I stand
upon Your promise that when I call upon You, You will not turn
away but will incline Your ear and deliver me from every trouble.

Lord, in every valley, in every midnight hour, and in every battle, I
know I am not alone. You are with me in the fire, You are with me
in the storm, and You are with me in the fight against my enemies.
Break the grip of every adversary that has risen against my
household. Scatter the works of the destroyer, and overthrow the
powers of darkness that contend for my life.

I decree that trouble will not consume me, for You are my Deliverer.
You not only rescue me but also honor me, lifting me up in the
presence of those who mocked and opposed me. Let my testimony
become a display of Your power, O God.

Father, cover my family with Your wings of safety, let no plague
come near us, and let no evil overpower us. Because You are with
us, we will not fear. Our deliverance is certain, and our victory is
secure. In Jesus' name, Amen.

DAY 24

LIFTED THROUGH HUMILITY

Humble yourselves in the sight of the Lord, and he will
exalt you.
—James 4:10 WEB

Exalted King of Glory, I bow low before You, acknowledging that
without You I am nothing. You are the lifter of heads, the One who
raises the poor from the dust and seats them among princes. Today,
I humble myself beneath Your mighty hand, seeking Your
deliverance from the snares of pride, arrogance, and every spirit
that opposes Your will in my life.

Lord, where the enemy has used pride to open doors of destruction,
I repent and surrender fully to You. Deliver me from every demonic
trap set to exploit my weaknesses. Tear down the altars of self that
empower the adversary, and let Your grace clothe me with strength.

Father, raise me up in Your timing. Lift my household into realms
of honor and breakthrough that only You can grant. Let the powers
of darkness see and tremble, for You exalt those who walk humbly
before You. Where the enemy sought to bring us low, let Your hand
elevate us to places of influence and peace.

I declare that our humility becomes a weapon of warfare, disarming
the schemes of the enemy. As I stay bowed before You, I rise in Your
authority. The forces of darkness are defeated, and Your glory
shines through my life.

In Jesus' name, Amen.

DAY 25

Judge My Cause, O Lord

Vindicate me, God, and plead my cause against an ungodly nation. Oh, deliver me from deceitful and wicked men.
—Psalm 43:1 WEB

Righteous Judge, I present my case before Your throne today. You are the God who defends the innocent and delivers the oppressed. Arise, O Lord, and plead my cause against every ungodly force, against every wicked adversary, and against every deceitful scheme set against me and my family.

Lord, where men have risen with lies, let their falsehood be exposed. Where wicked powers have conspired in secret, let their plans be overturned. Deliver me from the deceitful tongues that slander, from the manipulative hands that scheme, and from the oppressors that seek my downfall. You are my Advocate, and You will not allow the righteous to be condemned.

Father, stand as my Defender in every unseen courtroom of the spirit. Render judgment in my favor, and silence the accusations of the enemy. Let those who contend with my soul stumble and fall, and let Your justice shine forth like the noonday sun.

Today I declare that I am delivered from the grip of deceit and wickedness. My household is preserved under the covering of the blood of Jesus, and no lying tongue or evil work will prosper against us. You, O Lord, are our salvation, our vindication, and our strong Deliverer.

In Jesus' name, Amen.

DAY 26

STAND STILL AND SEE

Moses said to the people, "Don't be afraid. Stand still, and
see the salvation of Yahweh, which he will work for you
today; for the Egyptians whom you have seen today, you
shall never see them again."
—Exodus 14:13 WEB

Mighty Deliverer, I lift my voice today to declare that my enemies
will not have the last word over my life. You are the God who parts
seas, the One who dismantles armies, the Champion who stands
for His people when all seems lost. I refuse fear. I silence panic. I
stand still in the confidence of Your unfailing hand.

Lord, I decree that the forces arrayed against me and my family shall
not prevail. The strongholds of generational bondage, the pursuing
powers of darkness, the accusing spirits of the enemy—these
Egyptians of my soul—shall be buried by Your mighty salvation. I
do not tremble before them; I stand in the assurance of Your Word
that they shall be seen no more.

O Captain of Hosts, march before me. Drown the adversaries that
pursue my destiny in the depths of Your power. Just as Pharaoh's
chariots were swallowed up in the sea, let every demonic
assignment and evil counsel against my household perish in defeat.

I declare freedom, victory, and lasting deliverance. I stand firm,
clothed with courage, beholding the salvation You manifest. My

enemies are silenced forever, and my path is secured in Your covenant love.

In Jesus' name, Amen.

DAY 27

PRESERVED IN THE MIDST OF TROUBLE

Though I walk in the middle of trouble, you will revive me.
You will stretch out your hand against the wrath of my
enemies. Your right hand will save me.
—Psalm 138:7 WEB

O God of my salvation, I exalt You as the One who revives me in the very heart of battle. Even in the thick of trouble, when darkness presses in on every side, You breathe life into my spirit. You do not abandon me to the schemes of my adversaries. You stretch forth Your mighty right hand and shield me from the consuming wrath of the enemy.

Lord, I decree that every arrow of destruction hurled at my family is broken in midair. Every snare of the wicked is shattered. While trouble rages around me, it cannot consume me, for Your hand is upon me. Let Your saving strength dismantle the fury of evil powers that rise against my life.

Mighty Deliverer, silence the voices that mock my faith. Rebuke the destroyer who seeks to swallow my blessings. As You revive me, restore my courage, renew my joy, and strengthen my faith. I will not wither under pressure. I will not bow to fear. You uphold me with Your strong right hand, and none can snatch me from Your grasp.

I walk forward preserved, defended, and delivered. The trouble I see today will be turned into testimonies of triumph. Your saving hand secures me now and forever.

In Jesus' name, Amen.

DAY 28

My Rock and Fortress

He said, "Yahweh is my rock, my fortress, and my deliverer."
—2 Samuel 22:2 WEB

O Lord, my Rock and Deliverer, I proclaim Your greatness over my life. You are the immovable Rock beneath my feet, the fortress that shields me, the Deliverer who rescues me from every snare. I will not be shaken, for I am hidden in the stronghold of Your presence.

Lord, I declare that no enemy can penetrate the walls You have raised around me and my household. Every plan of darkness collapses before the fortress of Your power. My enemies may surround me, but they cannot overthrow me, for my life is fortified in You. I lean on You as my unshakable Rock; I run to You as my impenetrable Fortress.

You rescue me from hidden traps and overt attacks alike. No weapon formed against me prospers, for You deliver me out of them all. I proclaim that the powers of hell have no authority over my destiny. Their strongholds crumble before the Rock of Ages. Their plots dissolve in the fire of Your presence.

I rest secure in Your covenant love. You are my hiding place, my strength, my strong tower. I am preserved, defended, and upheld. In You, Deliverer of Israel, my victory is everlasting.

In Jesus' name, Amen.

DAY 29

Through the Waters and Flames

When you pass through the waters, I will be with you; and through the rivers, they will not overflow you. When you walk through the fire, you will not be burned, and flame will not scorch you.
—Isaiah 43:2 WEB

Faithful Father, I worship You as the God who walks with me through every trial. You never abandon me in deep waters; You never forsake me in the raging fire. You are my Deliverer, the One who shields me from destruction, the Keeper of my soul.

Lord, I decree that no flood of trouble will drown me or my family. Though rivers of adversity rise, they cannot sweep us away. Though flames of affliction rage, they cannot consume us. Your presence is my shield, Your Word my anchor, and Your Spirit my covering fire.

Every demonic flood seeking to overwhelm my destiny is restrained by Your power. Every fiery dart sent against my household is quenched by the fire of Your Spirit. I refuse fear; I embrace faith. I walk through the waters upheld, through the fire untouched, through the storm unbroken.

Almighty Deliverer, cover me with Your wings. Cause the very elements that sought to destroy me to become testimonies of Your deliverance. Let my life radiate the truth that You are with me in every season, carrying me to triumph.

In Jesus' name, Amen.

DAY 30

MY HIDING PLACE

You are my hiding place. You will preserve me from
trouble. You will surround me with songs of deliverance.
Selah.
—Psalm 32:7 WEB

O Lord, my Hiding Place, I run into the refuge of Your presence
today. You are the secret place where no arrow can touch me, no
curse can find me, no snare can hold me. You surround me with the
fortress of Your love and the shield of Your salvation.

Father, I declare that every plan of destruction against my
household is overturned. Trouble will not find me, for I am hidden
in You. Evil will not overtake me, for You preserve me by Your
mighty hand. Let every wicked plot be exposed and nullified, every
secret counsel of darkness be scattered by Your light.

Surround me, O Lord, with songs of deliverance. Let the melodies
of freedom silence the cries of oppression. Let the anthem of victory
ring louder than the accusations of the enemy. May my home
resound with testimonies of Your saving power, drowning out every
voice of fear and despair.

I rejoice in Your protection. I rejoice in Your deliverance. I declare
that my life and family are enveloped in an atmosphere of peace and
victory. I live hidden, preserved, and free, for You are my eternal
Hiding Place. In Jesus' name, Amen.

Epilogue

Deliverance is not the end of your story—it is the beginning of a new chapter marked by freedom, authority, and victory in Christ. Every prayer you have spoken, every Scripture you have declared, has not gone forth in vain. God's Word never returns empty; it accomplishes what He sends it to do.

As you step forward from these pages, carry this truth in your spirit: you are not a victim of the enemy's schemes—you are a victor through the blood of Jesus. The chains that once held you are broken. The fears that once silenced you are shattered. The enemies that once pursued you have been scattered by the hand of your Deliverer.

Now is the time to walk boldly in your freedom. Do not look back to Egypt; march forward into the promises God has prepared for you. Cover your family in prayer daily. Declare the Scriptures with authority. Stand firm in faith, knowing that the God who delivered you will continue to preserve and defend you.

Let songs of deliverance rise continually in your home. Let testimonies of rescue flow from your lips. And let your life be a living witness that the Lord is mighty to save.

The battle may rage, but your Deliverer reigns. Take your stand. Lift your voice. And live in the unshakable victory of Christ—today, tomorrow, and forever.

In Jesus' name, Amen.

Encourage Others with Your Story

If this prayer guide has strengthened your faith, deepened your intercession, or helped you stand in the gap, would you consider leaving a short review on Amazon? Your feedback not only encourages others but also helps more believers discover this resource and join in the prayer movement. Every review—just a few sentences—makes a difference. Thank you for being part of this movement.

MORE FROM PrayerScripts

COMMAND YOUR DESTINY SERIES

Command Your Morning:

30 Days of Prayers and Declarations to Seize Your Day and Shape Your Destiny

There is a battle over every morning—and every believer must choose to either drift into the day or command it.

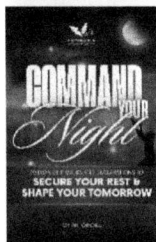

Command Your Night:

30 Days of Prayers and Declarations to Secure Your Rest and Shape Your Tomorrow

Every night is a spiritual battlefield—what you do before you sleep can determine the course of your tomorrow.

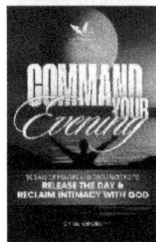

Command Your Evening:

30 Days of Prayers and Declarations to Release the Day and Reclaim Intimacy with God

There is a battle over every transition—and evening is one of the most spiritually neglected.

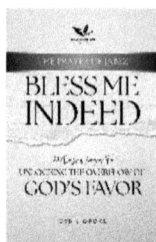

Bless Me Indeed:

Unlocking the Overflow of God's Favor

What if you could activate God's favor in your life today and walk in blessings that surpass your wildest expectations?

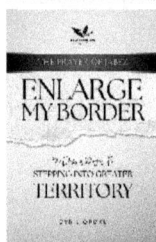

Enlarge My Border:

Stepping Into Greater Territory

Do you feel like you're living beneath your full potential? Do limitations, setbacks, and invisible barriers keep you from stepping into all God has promised? It's time to lift your cry for enlargement.

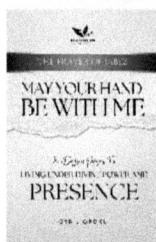

May Your Hand Be With Me:

Living Under Divine Power and Presence

What happens when the mighty hand of God rests upon your life? Doors open that no man can shut. Strength rises where weakness once prevailed. Guidance comes in the midst of confusion, and protection surrounds you in every battle.

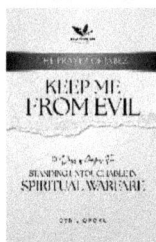

Keep Me From Evil:

Standing Untouchable in Spiritual Warfare

What if the enemy's plans could never touch you or your family? Imagine walking through life completely protected, untouchable, and victorious—no matter what schemes are formed against you.

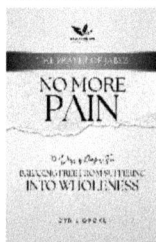

No More Pain:

Breaking Free from Suffering into Wholeness

Have you been carrying the weight of sorrow, disappointment, or hidden wounds for far too long? Do cycles of pain seem to repeat in your life, your marriage, or your family?

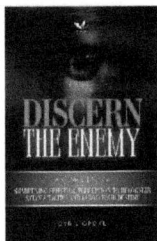

Discern the Enemy:

Sharpening Spiritual Perception to Recognize Satan's Tactics and Guard Your Destiny

The greatest danger is not the enemy you can see—it is the one you cannot. Can you recognize the enemy before he strikes?

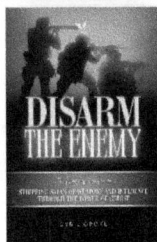

Disarm the Enemy:

Stripping Satan of Weapons and Influence Through the Power of Christ

Are you tired of feeling like the enemy has the upper hand in your life? It's time to take back your ground, silence the lies of darkness, and walk in the unstoppable authority of Christ.

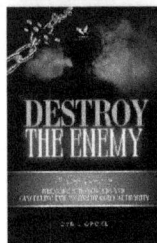

Destroy the Enemy:

Breaking Strongholds and Cancelling Evil Works by God's Authority

Are you tired of living under the weight of unseen battles? It's time to rise up and destroy the enemy's works in your life.

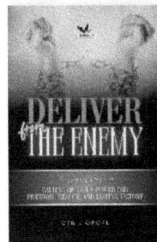

Deliver from the Enemy:

Calling on God's Power for Freedom, Rescue, and Lasting Victory

Break free from spiritual attacks and experience God's mighty deliverance in every battle.

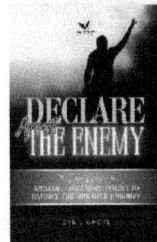

Declare Against the Enemy:

Speaking God's Word Boldly to Enforce Triumph Over Darkness

What if you could silence the enemy's schemes, protect your family, and walk boldly into every God-ordained assignment with unshakable authority?

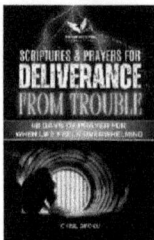

Scriptures & Prayers for Deliverance from Trouble:

40 Days of Prayer for When Life Feels Overwhelming

Are you walking through a season where life feels heavy and your prayers feel weak?

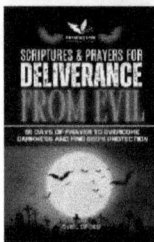

Scriptures & Prayers for Deliverance from Evil:

50 Days of Prayer to Overcome Darkness and Find God's Protection

When darkness presses in, how do you pray?

Scriptures & Prayers for Engaging the Enemy:

70 Days of Prayer to Rebuke the Enemy and Release God's Power

You weren't called to run from the battle—you were anointed to win it.

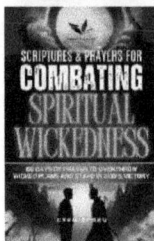

Scriptures & Prayers for Combating Spiritual Wickedness:

50 Days of Prayer to Overthrow Wicked Plans and Stand in God's Victory

Are you facing opposition that feels deeper than the natural? You're not imagining it—and you're not powerless.

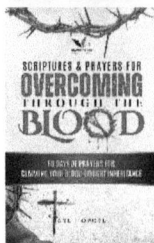

Scriptures & Prayers for Overcoming Through the Blood:

60 Days of Prayers for Claiming Your Blood-Bought Inheritance

You were never meant to fight sin, fear, or Satan in your own strength.

Standing in the Gap for Covenant Awakening:

30 Days of Prayer for National Repentance, Righteous Leadership & God's Sovereign Rule

What if your prayers could help turn the tide of a nation?

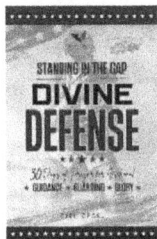

Standing in the Gap for Divine Defense:

30 Days of Prayer for National Guidance, Guarding & Glory

When the foundations of a nation feel as if they're shaking, prayer is the strongest fortress you can build.

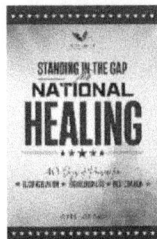

Standing in the Gap for National Healing:

40 Days of Prayer for Reconciliation, Righteousness, and Restoration

What if your prayers could help heal a nation? What if God is waiting for someone—like you—to stand in the gap?

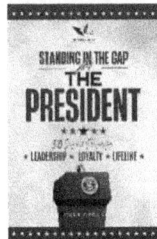

Standing in the Gap for The President:

50 Days of Prayer for Leadership, Loyalty, and Lifeline

When a nation's leader is under spiritual siege, will you answer the call to stand in the gap?

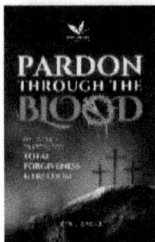

Pardon Through the Blood:

60 Days of Prayers for Total Forgiveness and Freedom

Guilt is a prison. The blood of Jesus holds the key.

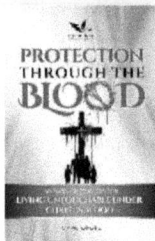

Protection Through the Blood:

60 Days of Prayers for Living Untouchable Under Christ's Blood

You are not helpless. You are not exposed. You are covered— completely—by the blood of Jesus.

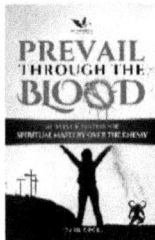

Prevail Through the Blood:

60 Days of Prayers for Spiritual Mastery Over the Enemy

What if every scheme of the enemy against your life could be dismantled—by one unstoppable weapon?

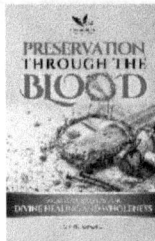

Preservation Through the Blood:

60 Days of Prayers for Divine Healing and Wholeness

Unlock Lasting Healing and Wholeness Through the Blood of Jesus

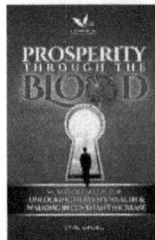

Prosperity Through the Blood:

60 Days of Prayers for Unlocking Heaven's Wealth and Walking in Covenant Increase

You were redeemed for more than survival—you were redeemed to prosper.

Peace Through the Blood:

60 Days of Prayers for Resting in the Covenant of Unshakable Peace

Are you ready to silence every storm of the mind, heart, and home—once and for all?